From: Aunt Cindy
5/99

Cornerstones of Freedom

The Story of

Malcolm X

Jack Slater

CHILDRENS PRESS®

CHICAGO

Library of Congress Cataloging-in-Publication Data

Slater, Jack.
  Malcolm X / by Jack Slater.
    p. cm. — (Cornerstones of freedom)
  Summary: Traces the life of the Black Muslim leader
who worked to foster self-respect among African
Americans.
  ISBN 0-516-06669-2
  1. X, Malcolm, 1925-1965—Juvenile literature.
2. Black Muslims—Biography—Juvenile literature.
3. Afro-Americans—Biography—Juvenile literature.
[1. X, Malcolm, 1925-1965. 2. Afro-Americans—
Biography.] I. Title. II. Series.
BP223.Z8L5775 1993
320.5'4'092—dc20   93-12687
[B]   CIP
                                                               AC

"**M**y black brothers and sisters—*no* one will know *who* we are . . . until *we* know who we are! We never will be able to *go* anywhere until we know *where* we are!"

That was one of Malcolm X's most important messages to African-American young people. He hammered it out again and again on street corners, in churches, on television and radio, and at many of the mass rallies held by the Black Muslims in the early 1960s.

"The black man," Malcolm X declared, "was . . . kidnapped from his homeland and stripped of his language, his culture, his family structure, his family name, until the black man in America [does] not even realize who he [is]."

Malcolm X speaking in Harlem, New York City, in 1961

Malcolm X always told African Americans that they must overcome the horrors of their past in order to find a better future. He also told them, "I don't think that anything is more positive than accepting what you are."

But he spoke differently to white people. With them, he used angry words that became weapons in his war against racism. "You have been as cold as an icicle whenever it came to the rights of the black man in this country," he once told a largely white audience at the Harvard Law School Forum. On an earlier occasion, he told the same group: "I don't come here tonight to speak to you as a Democrat or a Republican or an American or anything that *you* want me to be. I'm speaking as what I am: one of 22 million black people in this country who are victims of your democratic system."

A brilliant, articulate speaker, Malcolm X eloquently expressed the frustration and rage of blacks in America. Because he was so effective at using television and newspapers to hammer his message home, some people called him the "first of the media revolutionaries." But his radical views made him a controversial figure. The New

Malcolm X talking with reporters in New York City in 1964

York Police Department believed that he should be watched carefully. The Federal Bureau of Investigation called him a "menace."

African Americans saw Malcolm X quite differently. "He was able to cut down the enemy with his tongue—that was his excitement for black people," said the Reverend Jesse Jackson.

"Malcolm was our manhood, our living, black manhood. . . . Our own black shining prince!" declared actor Ossie Davis.

Young Malcolm and his family were well acquainted with despair, poverty, and violence. One night in 1925, a few weeks before Malcolm was born, a party of Ku Klux Klan riders

Klansmen parading through the streets of Tulsa, Oklahoma, in 1923

galloped up to his family's house in Omaha, Nebraska. Surrounding the house, the group demanded that Malcolm's father, the Reverend Earl Little, step outside. Louise Little, visibly pregnant with Malcolm, came outside to tell the Klan that her husband was out of town, preaching.

The Klan was an infamous, white-supremacist secret society that had terrorized blacks since 1866. The white-robed men who appeared at the Littles' house intended to stop Earl Little from preaching about black rights. As a member of Marcus Garvey's Universal Negro Improvement Association, Reverend Little urged African Americans to be proud of being black and to stop attempting to become a part of white society. Instead, he declared, they should leave America and establish a separate nation in Africa.

Marcus Garvey

Fearing the rise of black pride or black assertiveness, the Ku Klux Klan wanted to lynch Earl Little right there in front of his family. But since he wasn't home, the Klansmen rode around the house, frightened the family, and smashed windows. Then they warned Louise to tell her husband to get out of town. When Malcolm's father returned home, he realized he would have to move his family to a safer place. After Malcolm was born, the Little family moved to Milwaukee, Wisconsin. Later, they resettled in Lansing, Michigan.

In Lansing, Earl Little, a proud, determined man, continued with his attempts to organize African Americans under the principles of Garvey's back-to-Africa movement. Those efforts, however, were abruptly ended in 1929, when the Littles' home was again attacked by night riders. This time the riders, white supremacists who called themselves Black Legionnaires, burned the house down.

Malcolm, who was four years old at the time, would later recall the incident in his book *The Autobiography of Malcolm X:* "I remember being snatched awake into a frightening confusion of pistol shots and shouting and smoke and flames. My father had shouted and shot at the two white men who had set the fire and were running away. . . . I remember we were outside in the night in our underwear, crying and yelling our heads off. The white police and firemen came and stood around watching as the house burned down to the ground."

The Little family then moved to the outskirts of nearby East Lansing. Here, too, life became intolerable, because the family continued to be harassed. Moreover, as Malcolm later wrote, "In those days Negroes weren't allowed after dark in East Lansing proper." So the Little family moved again, this time to a rural area near East Lansing, into a four-room house that Earl Little built with his own hands.

Lansing as it looked when Malcolm's family lived there in the 1920s

But tragedy continued to dog the lives of the Littles. One bleak day in 1931, when Malcolm was six, his father was brutally murdered in Lansing, probably by members of the white Black Legion. With his skull shattered, he had been laid across trolley tracks for a streetcar to run over him. "His body was cut almost in half," Malcolm later recalled.

Now, in the heart of the Great Depression, when money and food were scarce, and many men couldn't find work, Malcolm's family struggled to survive without Earl Little. The money from one life insurance policy helped the family for a while. But the company that had issued the larger policy refused to pay off, claiming that Earl Little had committed suicide.

The Great Depression, which left thousands of Americans without jobs (above), hit the Little family particularly hard.

Some of the older children dropped out of school and found odd jobs around the area to help the family. Louise Little, a light-skinned woman, found work as a maid in the homes of several white families. However, she was always fired immediately after her employers discovered she was black. During this period, Malcolm and his brothers and sisters frequently sat down to a dinner that consisted of only boiled dandelion greens or cornmeal mush.

To help her family, Louise Little was forced to seek financial aid from the state welfare department. But help came too late for her. The pressure of providing for her eight children had begun to take its toll on her. Increasingly discouraged, she began to decline emotionally and mentally. "We children watched our anchor giving away," Malcolm later wrote. Finally, one day, after she was found wandering barefoot in the snow, Malcolm's mother was committed to a mental hospital. She remained there for twenty-six years.

In the meantime, Malcolm, nearly a teenager and already souring on life, began fighting with other youngsters in school. He also started turning over farmers' outhouses and stealing fruit and candy from local stores. The thefts got him in trouble with the police and the fighting led to his expulsion from school. Soon he found himself placed in a juvenile detention home in nearby Mason, Michigan. Here, under the supervision of a white couple named the Swerleins, Malcolm's behavior improved enormously. Enrolled in a largely white junior high school in Mason, he became a top student and was elected president of his eighth-grade class.

It seemed as if Malcolm had at last found a niche for himself. Yet the detention facility proved to be a mixed blessing. Malcolm later recalled that the Swerleins, though good people, "would . . . talk about me, or about 'niggers,' as though I wasn't there. . . . A hundred times a day, they used the word 'nigger.'"

About this time, during a summer vacation, he took a Greyhound bus east to Boston to visit his half-sister Ella Collins, a successful businesswoman and a child from his father's first marriage. The visit changed his life. He became

*Above: The junior high school that
Malcolm attended in Mason, Michigan
Right: Ella Collins, Malcolm's half-sister*

fascinated by the lure of the big city: the crowds, the diversions, the sheer size of Boston. In fact, he became so fascinated that a restlessness overtook him when he returned to Mason at the end of the summer.

One day, a teacher asked Malcolm what he wanted to do in life. He said he wanted to be a lawyer. "Malcolm," the teacher replied, "one of life's first needs is for us to be realistic. . . . A lawyer—that's no realistic goal for a nigger." The teacher told him he should instead become a carpenter.

From that moment on, Malcolm, who had achieved top grades, and who had believed he could indeed become a lawyer, became discouraged with school. He asked Ella Collins to let him come live with her in Boston. She agreed.

His move to Boston represented the end of one phase of his life and the beginning of another. The move took him on a downward spiral that led him through the mean streets of Boston's Roxbury section, into bars and dance halls and gambling dens.

Admitting that he wanted to "look white," he had his hair "conked"—straightened and dyed red with a scalp-burning mixture of Vaseline, lye, eggs, and potatoes. A tall, handsome youth with light-brown skin, he cultivated a "hip cat" image by donning the brightly colored "zoot suits" fashionable at the time and by spending evenings

Left: Boston as it looked when Malcolm moved there in the 1940s
Below: Teenagers wearing the "zoot suits" fashionable at the time

at nightclubs dancing the Lindy Hop, an energetic jitterbug of the period.

At sixteen, after landing a job as a sandwich man on passenger trains traveling the East Coast, Malcolm moved to New York City's Harlem, which was, he would later remember, "like some technicolor bazaar." In Harlem, he found the place "where I belonged." After quitting his job on the trains, he began to slide into a life of crime. He didn't worry that he might be headed down the wrong path, because he had come to believe that America offered no opportunities for young black men.

Because he hailed from Michigan, he became known on the streets as Detroit Red. It was under that nickname that he began selling dope, running numbers (collecting tickets for an illegal lottery game run by the mob), and procuring prostitutes in Harlem for white men. Eventually,

Malcolm at age eighteen, after being arrested in Boston for larceny

Charlestown Prison, where Malcolm served the first two years of his jail term

living in Harlem became too difficult and too dangerous for him. His life was threatened, so he returned to Boston, where, resuming his criminal activities, he began burglarizing homes of the wealthy. Inevitably, the police caught up with him. In early 1946, at the age of twenty, Malcolm Little found himself sentenced to ten years for burglary. "I had not even started shaving," Malcolm recalled in his autobiography.

Prison life for Malcolm was both terrible and wonderful, oppressive and, ultimately, life-giving. His term began in Massachusetts's Charlestown Prison, where he fought so hard against prison regulations that he came to be called Satan. He took drugs, he cursed guards, he threw things out of his cell, he refused to answer to his number.

He later recalled, "I would pace for hours like a caged leopard, viciously cursing aloud to myself." He had, as he said, "sunk to the very bottom of the American white man's society."

Even so, prison was where he struggled out of the straitjacket of that society. One of Malcolm's fellow inmates was an older, self-educated black man named Bimbi. The other prisoners would gather and listen, transfixed, when Bimbi talked about history and religion. "He was the first man I had ever seen command total respect . . . with his words," Malcolm wrote. One day, Bimbi told Malcolm flatly that he had some brains, if he'd use them. He advised Malcolm to take advantage of correspondence courses and the prison library.

Bimbi's words made an impression. Soon after, Malcolm began a correspondence course in grammar and writing. That represented his first step toward freedom. When he was transferred to Norfolk Prison in 1948, he took his second step. At the urging of his brothers and sisters, he began studying the teachings of a black religious group called the Nation of Islam. His siblings wrote him that this particular sect of Islam was "the natural religion for the black man."

The Nation of Islam, whose converts were known as Black Muslims, taught that the white man was the devil and that blacks were Allah's chosen people. The Black Muslims pointed to historical facts to bolster this claim by declaring

Norfolk Prison

A Nation of Islam meeting in the 1960s

that "history's greatest crime was the [slave] traffic in black flesh." Conducted by the white man for more than two centuries, the slave traffic brought millions of Africans in chains to the United States, where they were often worked to death, beaten, and tortured. Slavery ended with the Emancipation Proclamation in 1863. But, as the Muslims explained to Malcolm, injustices, lynchings, and racial inequality remained to destroy the black person's self-esteem. Malcolm learned that centuries of prejudice had caused African Americans to hate everything about themselves: their skin color, the texture of their hair, the thickness of their lips—their very existence.

In prison, Malcolm vowed to change all that. "In prison . . . I made up my mind to devote the rest of my life to telling the white man about himself." Also, the more he learned about the plight of the black man in America, the more he dedicated himself to broadening his knowledge of the world around him.

Painstakingly, he began copying the dictionary, page by page, because, as he said later, language became "an obsession with me." He joined the prison debating society. He read book after book: Will Durant's *Story of Civilization,* H. G. Wells's *Outline of History,* W. E. B. Du Bois's *Souls of Black Folk,* among others. And, most importantly, he began corresponding with Elijah Muhammad, leader of the Black Muslims.

In fact, with Malcolm's reading, debating, and correspondence, the years in prison passed so quickly that he was hardly aware of being locked up. In prison, he later declared, "I had never been so truly free in my life."

After serving about six and a half years of his sentence, Malcolm was released on parole in Detroit. The reddish conked hair had long since vanished, and he now wore glasses to correct an

Malcolm emerged from prison a changed man.

Malcolm X with Elijah Muhammad, the leader of the Nation of Islam

astigmatism he had developed by reading in the poor light of prison cells. Moreover, he had a new name. No longer Malcolm Little, he was now Malcolm X. "I dropped my slave name," he once explained. "I carry X because I don't know my real name." Out of prison in 1952, he went right into the awaiting arms of the Nation of Islam.

Because of his speaking ability, as well as his radiant intensity, he rose quickly through the ranks of the Muslim ministry. When he joined the Nation of Islam, it had about four hundred members. By 1960, Malcolm X had helped build the organization into a congregation of some ten thousand converts. For his efforts, he was awarded the pastorship of Mosque No. 7 in New York City.

A man selling Muhammad Speaks, the Black Muslim newspaper Malcolm X founded in 1957

Malcolm X became a prominent figure just as the Civil Rights Movement in America was gaining momentum. It was the early 1960s, a time when the nightly news often showed civil-rights demonstrators in the South being attacked and beaten by police. At times, as many as fifteen thousand African Americans would converge upon Harlem street rallies to hear Malcolm X declare in his rich, thrilling baritone: "You can't call a man defending his home a rioter. You can't call a man who is defending his babies and his children and his women a rioter. You call the rioter the one who is attacking—those white people down there [in Alabama], who are

Malcolm X speaking at a Harlem street rally in 1963

When out in public, Malcolm X was usually surrounded by an elite group of Black Muslims known as the Fruit of Islam.

policemen in uniform. The law itself is what is attacking our people and that law in Alabama could never attack black people unless the federal government of the United States condoned it."

Malcolm X's message differed from that of Martin Luther King, Jr., who believed that nonviolent protest was the best way to work toward racial equality. Malcolm X argued that violence—for self-protection—was acceptable, and disdained the integrationist policies favored by most civil-rights leaders. Instead, he advocated a revolutionary program that called for a separate nation—free from white

Martin Luther King, Jr., and Malcolm X

domination—for blacks. A woman who observed
Malcolm during that period said of him: "He was
the protector. It was like you knew you had a big
brother at home who could knock down anybody
who messed with you."

While Malcolm frightened many white people,
he was also beginning to alarm some black
people, particularly Muslims who were close to
Elijah Muhammad. Malcolm's growing
popularity outside Muslim circles was the source
of considerable irritation to some of Messenger
Muhammad's advisers. They wanted Malcolm not
only disciplined, but muzzled, even silenced.

Finally, in November 1963, when President John F. Kennedy was assassinated, Muhammad's advisers got their wish. Malcolm had publicly described the assassination as an example of "the chickens coming home to roost"—meaning that whites were finally paying the price for having established a climate of hate in America. But Malcolm's remarks made Elijah Muhammad furious. "That was a very bad statement," he told Malcolm. "The country loved this man. . . . I'll have to silence you for the next ninety days, so that Muslims everywhere can be disassociated from the blunder."

As it turned out, that ninety-day suspension was the beginning of the end of Malcolm's

Aware that he had many enemies, Malcolm X was always looking over his shoulder.

During his suspension, Malcolm tried to relax by taking his family to the Miami boxing camp of his friend, Cassius Clay (Muhammad Ali).

association with the Nation of Islam. Eventually, he saw that the Muslim inner circles really did not want his presence anymore. After a series of painful, personal decisions, he reluctantly separated himself altogether from the organization. For a dozen years, the Nation of Islam had been the entire meaning of his life. Exhausted, uncertain of his future outside the Nation, Malcolm looked around him and wept. "He shed tears," one of his closest friends sadly recalled.

He put his energy into founding two organizations: Muslim Mosque, Inc., and, later, the Organization of Afro-American Unity (OAAU). The OAAU was set up to foster unity

Malcolm X making his first speech after his break with the Nation of Islam in March 1964

between Africans and black Americans. Malcolm X intended the Muslim Mosque group to help the American black urban community gain political and economic control of its own affairs. He called such control "black nationalism," a phrase that would later become "Black Power" under younger activists such as Stokely Carmichael. Malcolm insisted that African Americans could— and should—control their own communities. It was simply a matter of regaining one's self-respect, he said. "That's what black nationalism *is*—personal pride."

Worshipers in Mecca, Saudi Arabia, the holy city of Islam

Having left the Nation of Islam, Malcolm X now became interested in the religion from which it had sprung—orthodox Islam. He learned that in traditional Islamic faith, as practiced in the Middle East, people are judged not by their color, but by their actions. He began to realize that some of the separatist racial doctrines of the Black Muslims contradicted orthodox Islamic teachings.

In April 1964, Malcolm X traveled to the Middle East on a pilgrimage to Mecca, the holy city of Islam. There, to his amazement, he found white people breaking bread with people whose skin was black and brown and yellow. "I found myself," Malcolm remembered, "drinking from the same glass, and sleeping on the same cot, and praying on the same rug with people who in this country would definitely be classified as white people."

Malcolm could hardly believe what he was seeing. "To me," he recalled later, "a white man had always been a *white man*—this was my blanket classification. But I had to finally reach the conclusion that [what made the white people in Mecca] different . . . was the fact that they had accepted the oneness of God, and in accepting the oneness of God, their intelligence demanded that they also accept the oneness of humanity."

Malcolm X meeting with Muslim leaders in Cairo, Egypt, in July 1964

Malcolm with daughter Ilyasah

Mecca had been a kind of paradise on earth for Malcolm. It inspired him to modify his views on black separatism, and begin to imagine the possibility of world brotherhood. When he returned home to the United States, however, he confronted the usual racial problems. Now, in addition, a religious war awaited him. The Nation of Islam still had not forgiven him for daring to leave the congregation or for starting a new Muslim organization. It set about to assure his destruction.

Malcolm X arrives to inspect the damage to his house after it was firebombed on February 14, 1965.

On February 14, 1965, Malcolm's home in Queens, New York, was firebombed. The incident reminded him of another firebombing thirty-five years earlier. Once again, a wife and children, his own, were snatched awake into a frightening confusion of shouting and smoke and flames.

Malcolm and his family survived, but the end for him was near. "I'm no stranger to danger," he said. "I have lived with danger all my life. I never expect to die of old age. I know that I have done the very best that I could for our people."

The last known portrait taken of Malcolm X

On February 21, 1965, the Sunday following the destruction of his home, Malcolm X entered New York City's Audubon Ballroom to make a speech. He was tired that day, and worried about the threats made on his life. But at the podium, he smiled broadly and looked out at the large audience before uttering the Islamic greeting, "*As salaam alaikum*, brothers and sisters." And the audience responded, "*As alaikum salaam*."

At that instant, eight rows of seats from the stage, a man suddenly stood up and shouted, "Take your hand out of my pocket!" The audience turned to look at the disturbance. "Hold it! Hold it!" Malcolm said from the podium. "Don't get excited. Let's cool it, brothers."

Then, with the audience distracted, three gunmen in the front row stood and started firing simultaneously at Malcolm. "It looked like a firing squad," one witness recalled.

The Audubon Ballroom just after the assassination of Malcolm X

*Betty Shabazz,
Malcolm's widow*

Clutching his chest, Malcolm fell back, knocking over two chairs as his bloodied head struck the floor of the stage. In the pandemonium that followed the shooting, Malcolm was rushed to Columbia-Presbyterian Hospital, but he was dead before he reached the emergency operating room.

He was thirty-nine years old.

Eventually, three black men, all Muslims, were convicted of the murder of Malcolm X and sentenced to life in prison. Two of them later left prison on parole. But the third man soon confessed that the other two had been innocent and that Malcolm's murder had been plotted by five Muslims.

People throughout the world mourned the death of Malcolm X. African Americans realized that his great gift to this country was his boundless love for black persons. "He believed in their beauty and their possibilities and tried to make them believe, too," said Peter Goldman, one of Malcolm's biographers. "But his more important legacy was his example, his bearing, his affirmation of blackness—his understanding that one is paralyzed for just so long as one believes one cannot move."

Malcolm X in 1963

Thousands lined the streets to say farewell after Malcolm X's funeral.

INDEX

PHOTO CREDITS

Cover, 1, © Robert L. Haggins; 2, AP/Wide World; 3, UPI/Bettmann; 4, 5, © Robert L. Haggins; 6, AP/Wide World; 7, Stock Montage; 9, State Archives of Michigan; 10, Stock Montage; 12, (left), Dembinsky Photo Assoc.; 12 (right), UPI/Bettmann; 13 (left), The Bostonian Society; 13 (right), UPI/Bettmann; 14, unknown photographer; 15, 16, 17, UPI/Bettmann; 18, 19, Schomburg Center for Research in Black Culture; 20 (top), UPI/Bettmann; 20 (bottom), AP/Wide World; 21 (top), © Robert L. Haggins; 21 (bottom), UPI/Bettmann; 22, 23, 24, © Robert L. Haggins; 25, UPI/Bettmann; 26, SuperStock; 27, 28 (both photos), UPI/Bettmann; 29, © Robert L. Haggins; 30 (both photos), AP/Wide World; 31 (both photos), UPI/Bettmann

Picture Identifications:
Cover: Malcolm X at a Harlem street rally in June 1963
Page 1: Malcolm X with his daughters Qubilah and Attalah
Page 2: Malcolm X speaking at a rally in 1963

Project Editor: Shari Joffe
Designer: Karen Yops
Photo Research: Jan Izzo
Cornerstones of Freedom Logo: David Cunningham

ABOUT THE AUTHOR

Jack Slater was born in Dayton, Ohio. He earned a degree in journalism from Temple University in Philadelphia and subsequently worked as a reporter-editor for *Ebony* magazine, *The New York Times Magazine*, and the *Los Angeles Times*. His work has also appeared in *Rolling Stone, Essence, California*, and *The New York Times Book Review*. He divides his time between Los Angeles and the mountain town of San Miguel de Allende, Mexico.

Like many young African Americans of the early 1960s, Mr. Slater was an admirer of Malcolm X. "While he lived, Malcolm X's influence was broad," says Mr. Slater. "In death, his influence is beyond measure."